The Shliach Who Worked in a Brush Factory

Written by
Rabbi Sholom Ber Zimmerman
Illustrated by
Ricky Audi

First published Tishrei 2022

Written by Rabbi Sholom Ber Zimmerman
Illustrated by Ricky Audi
Interior page design Bryony van der Merwe

MyRebbeArt@gmail.com

This book is dedicated to my parents
Yale & Chaya Rochel Zimmerman for
teaching me how to be a
shliach of the Rebbe.

The Parents

The Grandparents

One night, Zelig was settling down for a bedtime story, when his grandfather sat down with an old, yellowed letter in his hand.

"What's that, Zaidy?" asked Zelig.

"It's tonight's story," he replied. "This one is **very special** to me, because this is a **true story,"** Zaidy said, pulling the blanket over Zelig. "It's my story and my tatty's story, and that makes it your story, too!"

"That's my great-grandfather, Avraham Moshe, right?" Zelig asked.

Zaidy nodded and began his story.

"Long before you were born, when I was just a Tatty and Bubby was just a Mommy, **we dreamed of going on Shlichus** to spread Torah and teach mitzvos."

"We needed to decide where we would live and raise our family, but we didn't know which community would need us most, so we asked the Rebbe for help."

Zelig listened carefully. He imagined all the faraway cities he could live in someday. He wasn't sure where he would live when he grew up, but he hoped that one day he would have a **chabad house** of his own.

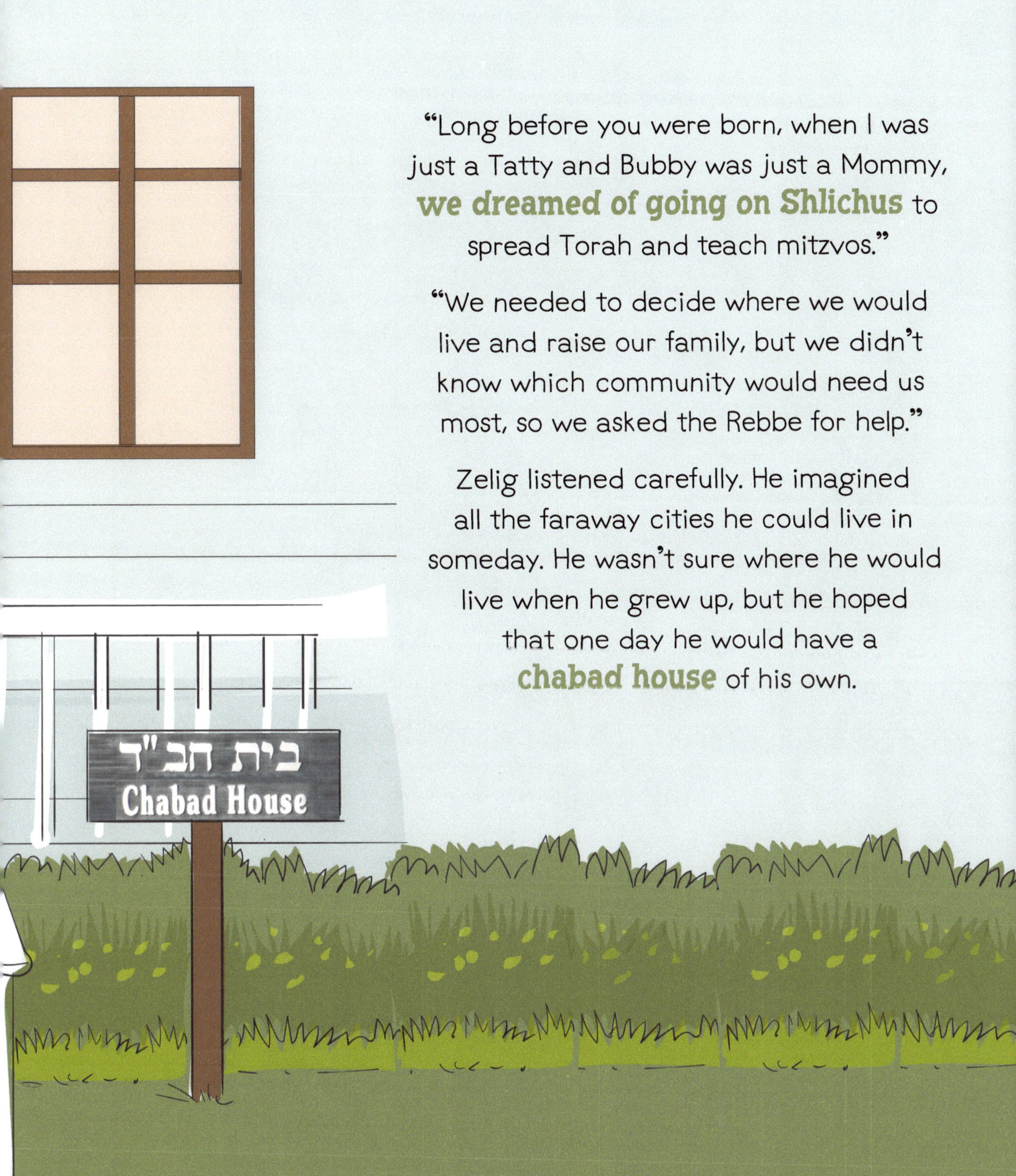

"The Rebbe was very **busy learning Torah** and **helping people.** He didn't have time to meet with us to help us decide. Can you guess how we asked for advice?" Zelig's grandfather asked.

"The letter!"

Zelig grinned.

He looked over Zaidy's shoulder and, through sleepy eyes, he read the list of cities across America where they had been invited to serve the Jewish communities.

Zelig was **amazed** by all the **different locations.**

He imagined his ducks with tiny sunglasses driving around **sunny California** and inviting Jewish men, women and children into their very own Chabad house.

Zelig imagined them helping at summer camps and watching sunsets by **the lake in Ohio.**

He pictured his ducks exploring the **parks of New Jersey,** and learning with all the yeshiva bochurim.

“But Zaidy,” Zelig said, “you never lived in any of those places.”

“Well, Zelig, this is where there is a twist in the story.” Zaidy unfolded the bottom of the page to reveal one last option:

the family business.

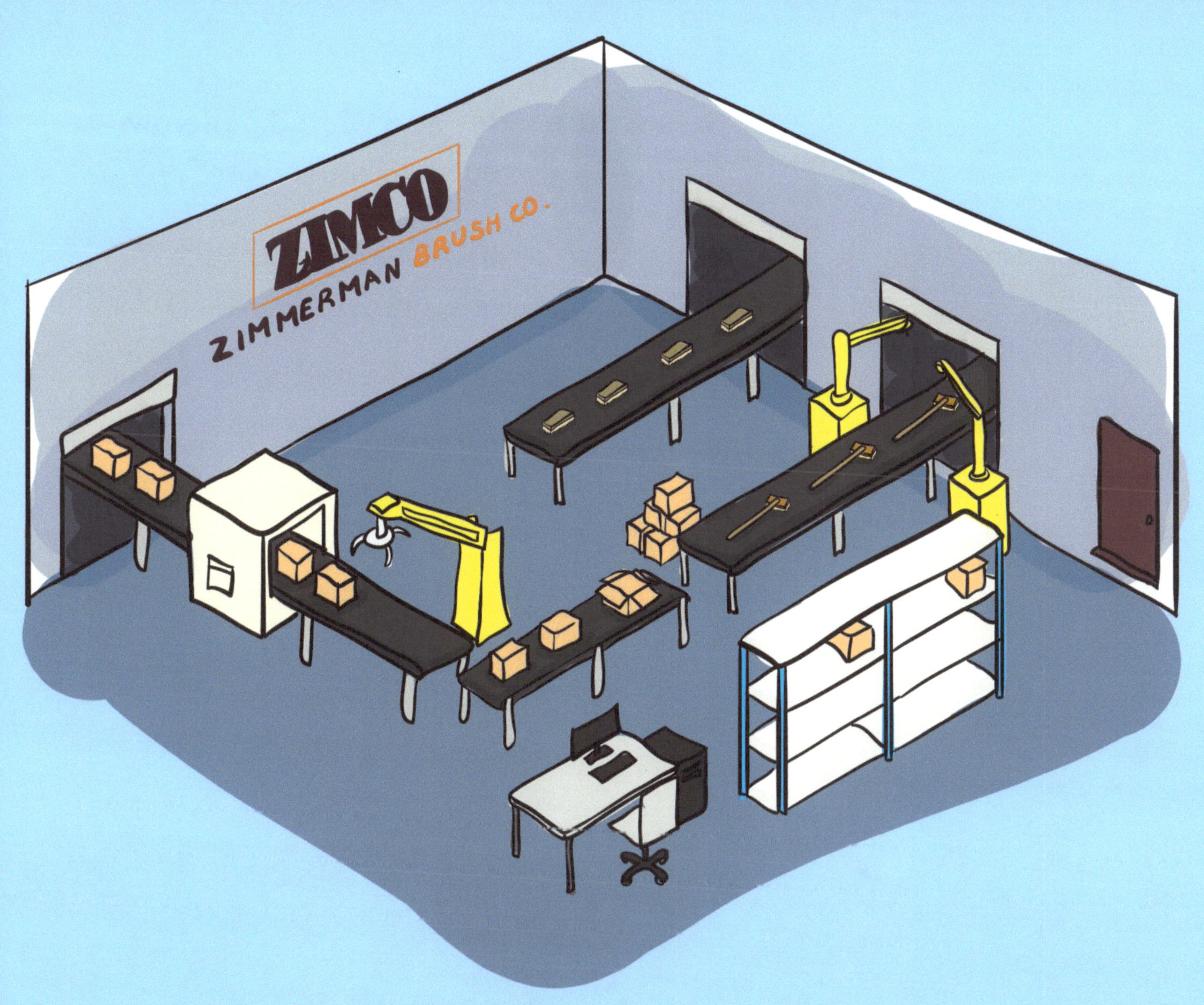

"My own Tatty, Mike, owned a **brush factory.** He had built it with his own hands from nothing after he immigrated from Poland. When I grew up and married your Bubby, he asked me to help with the family business," explained Zaidy. "Your great-grandfather was not frum, and he did not understand the importance of Shlichus. Even though we were sure it was our **life's mission** to help another community far away, we agreed to add it to our list."

"We sent the letter and waited patiently. Finally, we received an answer."

"Which one did the Rebbe pick?"
Zelig asked, his eyes wide.

"Can you guess?" Zaidy asked with a smile.

Zelig considered the choices. He looked at his ducks for help, but they stared back at him blankly. Zelig didn't know what the Rebbe would possibly decide when there were **so many options.**

"I'll tell you," said Zaidy. "The Rebbe chose the very last option: **the brush factory.**"

"Really?" Zelig gasped. "But surely the Rebbe would want you to start a shul or help people learn about yiddishkeit or...or.."

Zaidy interrupted, "This is what we expected as well, but a chassid **always listens to the Rebbe,** no matter what, even if we don't understand."

"Every person has a **specific job** in life." explained Zaidy. "The Rebbe wrote in Hayom Yom that Hashem gives you talents designed specifically for your mission. Therefore, instead of copying other people, you need to think, 'What am I good at?' If you try to do something that's not right for you, you could be wasting **the gifts Hashem has given you."**

"And that's what happened to us, The Rebbe recognized our unique abilities and sent us on a **Shlichus that was perfect for us.** Later that year, we moved to Chicago and I started work alongside your great-grandfather in the brush factory," Zaidy said.

"But our story does not end there. It took a lot of convincing, but your great-grandfather agreed to close the factory on Shabbos and Yom Tov. Eventually, he even let me **put tefillin on him** every day!" Zaidy said with a big smile.

ZIMCO
ZIMMERMAN BRUSH CO.
900
WEST LAKE STREET
SORRY WE ARE CLOSED FOR SHABBOS!

"Over time, we realized that just because we don't have a Chabad house doesn't mean we couldn't **spread yiddishkeit** like the Rebbe asks of us."

Zimmerman Brush Co

"We gave shiurim for men and women in our house and we **helped start a Jewish cheder,** too!" exclaimed Zaidy.

"That's my school!" Zelig smiled proudly. "You thought you weren't going on Shlichus when you went to work in the brush factory, but you really did!"

"That's right!" Zaidy said, straightening Zelig's yarmulke. "When the Rebbe chose the brush factory, we were as surprised as you were. But **the Rebbe helped us understand** that running a business did not mean putting a stop to spreading yiddishkeit, learning torah in our free time, and **inspiring everyone** we meet," Zaidy explained.

"We focused on the business, but we also helped to **change the world** for the better. So you see, the Rebbe **did** send us on Shlichus, even though it was not to a chabad house.

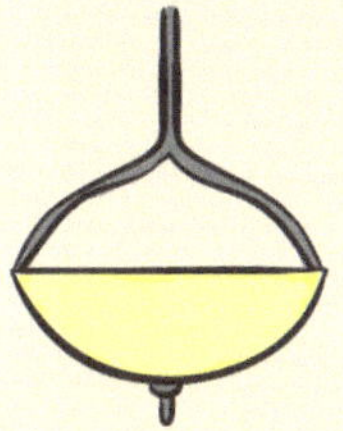

"So, the Rebbe was **right all along!"** Zelig jumped up in his bed in excitement.

"Exactly," his grandfather laughed. "The Jewish community in Chicago got **bigger and stronger,** and so did our family. We now have eleven children of our own, not to mention over forty grandchildren, including you! And when your time comes, your Shlichus will match with the **abilities that Hashem has given you."**

OFFICE

As Zelig hugged his Zaidy, he wondered if people driving by the brush factory ever realized how special it was on the inside. From the outside, it looked like any other ordinary factory. They would have no idea **it had shluchim inside.**

Zelig imagined all the businesses around the world that might share this **same secret.** He realized there could be hundreds of factories or offices **spreading the light of Torah and chassidus** just like his Zaidy's.

"Now this is your story, Zelig," Zaidy said as he kissed Zelig on his head and watched his grandson's eyes slowly flutter shut. "We don't know yet what you'll do, or where you'll live, but we do know that no matter what, you will use your unique talents to help **bring Mashiach closer."**

Zelig drifted off to sleep
dreaming of all the possibilities.

www.ingramcontent.com/pod-product-compliance
Lightning Source LLC
LaVergne TN
LVHW071109160826
845679LV00004B/1020
9798846672956